Illustrated
Stories *from the* Bible

Volume 9

AUTHORS
George and Marilyn Durrant
Former Professor of Ancient Scriptures

Doctor of Education

ARTIST AND ART DIRECTOR
Vernon Murdock
Artist Illustrator

Bachelor of Fine Arts
Graduate Work, University of Madrid,
    Spain

CORRELATORS AND DIRECTORS
Steven R. Shallenberger, *President*
Community Press, Eagle Marketing
    Corporation

Bachelor of Science; Accounting, Business
SCMP, Graduate School of Business, Harvard
    University

Paul R. Cheesman
Director of Scripture in Religious Study Center
Chaplain, U.S. Navy

Doctor of Religious Education

Lael J. Woodbury
Chairman, National Committee on Royalties,
    American Theatre Association

Doctor of Philosophy, University of Illinois

ADVISORS
Dale T. Tingey
Director of American Indian Services and
    Research Center

Doctor of Philosophy, Guidance and
    Counseling; Washington State University

Reverend Raymond E. Ansel
Ordained Minister

Southwestern Assemblies of God College, Texas
Berean Bible School, Missouri

Millie Foster Cheesman
Writer, Poetess

Reverend William R. Schroeder
United Church of Christ

United Theological Seminary of the Twin Cities
    New Brighton, Minnesota

The Woman saith unto him, I know that Messias cometh, which is called Christ: when he is come, he will tell us all things.

Jesus saith unto her, I that speak unto thee am he.

And many more believed because of his own word;

And said unto the woman, Now we believe, not because of thy saying: for we have heard him ourselves, and know that this is indeed the Christ, the Saviour of the world.

John 4:25, 26, 41, 42

Dedicated to boys and girls throughout the world
and to all who love the Bible.

A nondenominational work.

CONTENTS

Our story so far . . .

Much happened after Adam and Eve left the Garden of Eden. Over the years, although many people forgot the Lord, the Bible shows that the Lord never forgot his people. One way in which he blessed their lives was to send them great prophets. Through these holy and inspired servants, God sent eternal principles and commandments to teach his children how to gain peace in this life and eternal happiness in the life to come.

Yet, even with these righteous leaders, there was no life so good, no sacrifice so great, no love so complete as that of a man called Jesus. For it was this man, the Son of God, who was the fulfillment of all that the prophets had been teaching the children of Israel.

In Volume Nine we will learn more of the important lessons of Jesus' parables, and through their explanations we will be able to better understand his teachings. We will see the hate and jealousy of the religious leaders, who sensed that Jesus threatened their power over the people. As these evil men continued to plan his death, Jesus went forward with his work, teaching his Father's eternal plan of salvation, performing miracles, and training a group of men to continue on with his work after his crucifixion.

LOVE THY NEIGHBOR
The Parable of the Good Samaritan

People walked for miles to hear more of Jesus' teachings. When they asked him questions, he often answered them by telling a parable. A parable is a story that is easy to understand and teaches a simple truth.

"I have a question," shouted a lawyer, as he stood up only a short distance from Jesus.

"Master, what shall I do to inherit eternal life?" (Luke 10:25).

Jesus calmly asked, "What have you read in the scriptures about the answer to your question?"

The lawyer boldly replied, "The scriptures say I should love God and my neighbor."

Jesus replied, "Thou hast answered right. . . . " (Luke 10:28)

The lawyer, trying to catch Jesus in a mistake, smugly asked, "And who is my neighbor?" (Luke 10:29)

Jesus answered the man by telling him this parable:

9

"As a traveler was making a journey from Jerusalem to Jericho, he was suddenly attacked by a band of thieves. These evil men stole all the man's clothing and possessions and left him badly wounded.

"Shortly after this incident occurred, a priest passed by. When this religious leader, who was supposed to be a good man, saw the wounded traveler, he crossed over to the other side of the road and passed by without helping him.

"Later a Levite (a man who worked in God's temple) came to the same place. Seeing the wounded man, he became frightened and hurried past.

"But when a Samaritan came to where the man was lying, he felt compassion for him.

"Kneeling beside the wounded man, he used part of his own clothing to bandage up the man's wounds. The Samaritan then set the man on his donkey and led him to an inn some miles away. There he cared for him.

"The next day before leaving, the Samaritan gave the innkeeper some money and asked him to take care of the wounded man, adding that if it should cost more, he would repay him on his next trip."

Looking out through the crowd at the lawyer, Jesus spoke again.

Which now of these three, thinkest thou, was neighbour unto him that fell among the thieves?

And he [the lawyer] said, He that shewed mercy on [helped] him. Then said Jesus unto him, Go, and do thou likewise.

Luke 10:36, 37

When the parable was finished, a little boy looked up at his mother and asked, "Mother, did Jesus mean that we are all neighbors, even if we don't really live near someone, and even if we don't like a person?"

His mother replied, "That is exactly what he meant!"

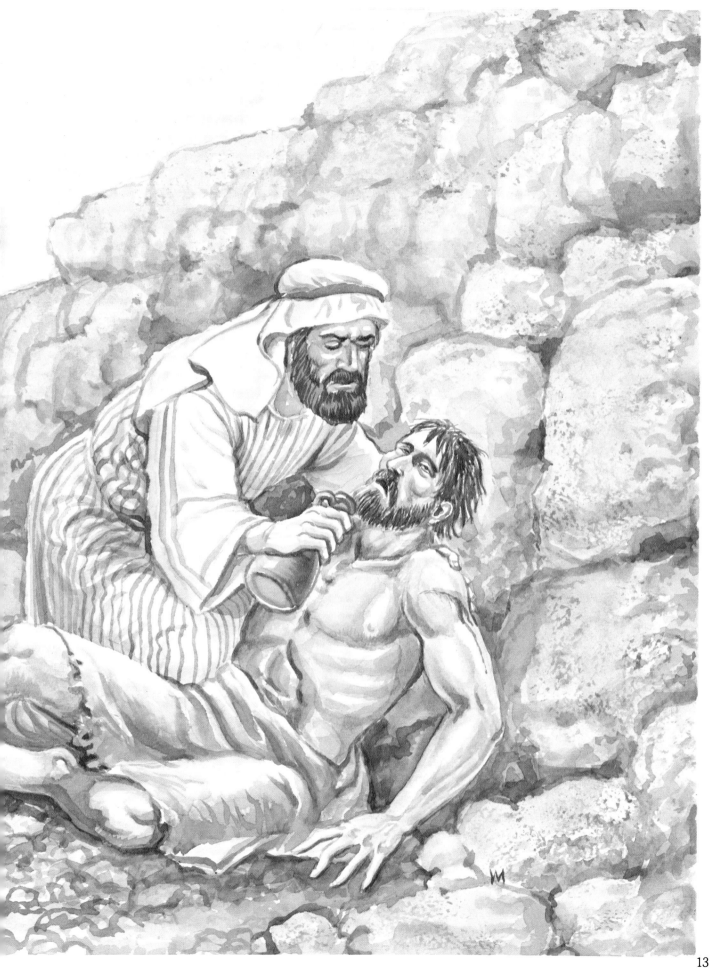

THE LORD IS OUR SHEPHERD
The Parable of the Lost Sheep

One day Jesus overheard the scribes and Pharisees murmuring against him because he taught publicans and sinners. This prompted Jesus to relate a short parable about sheep.

> What man of you, having an hundred sheep, if he lose one of them, doth not leave the ninety and nine in the wilderness, and go after that which is lost, until he find it?
>
> And when he hath found *it*, he layeth *it* on his shoulders, rejoicing.
>
> And when he cometh home, he calleth together *his* friends and neighbours, saying unto them, Rejoice with me; for I have found my sheep which was lost.

Luke 15:4-6

A nonbelieving listener whispered to his friend, "Why does he look at me when he speaks of lost sheep? I have no sheep. How can I look for lost sheep when I am a fisherman?"

The other spoke up and asked, "Master, you were speaking about sinners, and then you changed the subject to lost sheep. We do not understand!"

Jesus patiently explained that a sinner is like a sheep that is lost in the wilderness. When a person follows Satan, he wanders away from God's flock and becomes lost.

Then the man who had just asked Jesus the question said, "So sinners are to God as lost sheep are to the shepherd. The shepherd, or God, must seek them out and bring them back."

Jesus smiled approvingly and explained that just as the shepherd rejoices over finding a lost sheep, so does God rejoice when a sinner repents and comes back into his fold.

He then said, ". . . joy shall be in heaven over one sinner that repenteth, more than over ninety and nine just persons, which need no repentance." (Luke 15:7)

Jesus loves all people, and he knows that most of us are in some ways "lost sheep." Therefore, whenever we follow the teachings of Jesus, God and his angels are happy and rejoice over our good deeds.

THINK ABOUT IT

1. Who are the sheep in this parable? Who is the Shepherd?
2. Thinking about your answers, explain in your own words how parables have two meanings.

COME HOME TO GOD
The Parable of the Prodigal Son

Jesus' parables might be compared to diamond mines—there are treasured jewels (lessons) to be found in them. The parable of the Prodigal (wasteful and reckless) Son is a jewel because it shows God's great love for each of us.

Jesus wanted his disciples and all people everywhere to understand that often in life we do things that are wrong and make ourselves and others miserable. In this parable Jesus reminds us that if we have acted foolishly and have strayed from God's teachings, it is still not too late to return to our former good habits. Through repentence we can change and start over again on a new path. We can help those whom we have hurt and teach others not to make the same mistakes we have made. We can believe and trust in Jesus Christ and set out upon the road that will lead to peace, happiness, and eternal life. It was for this reason that Jesus came to earth, that we might change our ways and follow him.

On a certain day many followers had gathered expecting to hear Jesus teach a great lesson. No one left disappointed that day.

Jesus began:

"There was a man who had two sons. One day the younger of the two said to his father, 'Father, give me that which I am to inherit.' The father divided his wealth and gave each son his portion.

"A few days later the younger son took his inheritance and journeyed to a distant country. Within only a few weeks he had spent all his money on items of no value.

"At this time there arose a terrible famine in the land. There was not much food and, not having money to purchase any himself, the young man became extremely hungry.

"He searched for a job that would pay him enough to buy food, but there weren't any. In desperation he went to a farmer and begged, 'Please, sir, give me work of any kind.'

"The farmer, feeling sorry for this starving young man, said, 'Go into my fields and feed my pigs.'

"The young man's first thought was to turn down the offer, for such a job was thought to be disgraceful by his people. But feeling weak and hungry, he accepted.

"While feeding the pigs, he thought to himself, 'Although this food is only fit for pigs, I must eat it or I will die.'

"After eating all he could, he sat down a short distance from the hungry hogs and watched them as they ate their fill. As he sat, he thought of his home and his parents. He remembered how good life had once been to him and came to realize what a mistake it had been to leave home. He thought to himself, 'How many hired servants of my father's have bread enough and to spare, and I perish with hunger!' (Luke 15:17)

"Looking up at the first stars of the night, he resolved in his mind,

I will arise and go to my father, and will say unto him, Father, I have sinned against heaven, and before thee,

And am no more worthy to be called thy son: make me as one of thy hired servants.

Luke 15:18, 19

"With this firm resolve, he began the long journey home.

"Sometime later this young man was walking the last stage toward home. While yet a long ways off, his father saw him approaching. Running to meet him, the father embraced his son and kissed him.

And the son said unto him, Father, I have sinned against heaven, and in thy sight, and am no more worthy to be called thy son.

But the father said to his servants, Bring forth the best robe, and put *it* on him; and put a ring on his hand, and shoes on *his* feet:

And bring hither the fatted calf, and kill *it*; and let us eat, and be merry.

Luke 15:21-24

"When his elder brother came in from the field that day and heard the music and dancing, he asked why they were celebrating.

"The servant told him about his brother's return, and that his father had ordered a celebration party.

"The older brother was hurt and would not go into the house. When his father was told of this, he came out and asked what the matter was.

"His son answered, 'Father, all these many years I have served you and never did anything except that which would please you. But not once did you ever give me a goat, that I might make merry and have a feast with my friends:

"'Yet as soon as my younger brother, who has been away living a life of sin, returns home, you kill the fatted calf and have a big celebration.'

"The father waited until he was sure the oldest son had said all he wanted to say. Then he put his arm about him and spoke:"

Son, thou art ever with me, and all that I have is thine.

It was meet [appropriate] that we should make merry, and be glad: for this thy brother [was as if he] was dead, and [now he] is alive again; and [he] was lost, and [now he] is found.

Luke 15:31, 32

THINK ABOUT IT:

1. If the prodigal son had been your brother, would you have gone into the feast? Why?
2. Could we relate the father in this story to our Father in heaven? How?
3. In what ways might we be a little like the prodigal son?

27

HELPING THE LORD
The Parable of the Talents

As a family hurried through the city to hear Jesus speak, the oldest son lingered behind to look at a large, beautiful building.

The father, returning to where the boy stood, asked, "What are you looking at? Don't you know we must hurry?"

"I'll come now, Father, but I've never seen such an elegant building. Just look at it."

"Yes, indeed," the father said admiringly. "The finest builders in the land combined their talents to build such a thing of beauty."

As the two hurried to catch up with the rest of the family, the young man exclaimed in excitement, "Father, I like to build things."

"I know you do, and you have a talent for it," replied his father.

"What is a talent?" asked the boy.

The father explained: "A talent is having the ability to do something well. As you grow older, you try to improve this ability. For example, you have a talent for building things; others may have a talent to teach, write, paint, sing, sew, or repair things well."

It was several moments before the son finally spoke again. "I'd like to develop my talent and learn how to build beautiful buildings like the one we just passed."

Placing a hand on his son's shoulder, the father proudly replied, "That would please me, my son. Although God gave you the talent, you must develop it by working and learning. Then, if you use your talent to benefit those around you, God will be pleased."

Soon the family came upon a crowd of people listening to the words of Jesus. As they sat down, the young boy and his father were surprised to hear Jesus talking about talents. He seemed to be speaking of talents as if they were a type of money. Yet, in the young boy's mind he was thinking about the kind of talent needed to build a building, to play beautiful music, or to be a friendly person.

Jesus began a parable: He suggested to his listeners that they might compare the kingdom of heaven to a man who is about to go on a long journey. Just before he is to leave, he calls his servants to him and gives them everything he owns.

To one servant he gives five talents, to another servant he gives two talents, and to yet another he gives one talent. To each servant he gives the number of talents he feels that particular servant can best use. After he has done these things, he departs on his long journey.

Within several days the servant with five talents decides he must use his talents. Leaving home, he walks to the marketplace. There among the other men he uses his talents by trading with them. After a time of wisely buying and selling with his talents, he finds he has made a profit, so that now he not only has his first five talents but an additional five as well.

Meanwhile, the servant who has received two talents acts similarly. Going to the city, he manages his two talents wisely and makes a profit of two additional talents.

However, the servant who has received one talent, fearing he will lose it, buries it in the earth.

Many months later the master returns. Sending a message to each servant, he asks them to come and give an account of what they have done with the talents he has given them.

The servant who received the five talents excitedly reports to his master what he has done.

Lord, thou deliveredst unto me five talents: behold, I have gained beside them five talents more.

His lord said unto him, Well done, *thou* good and faithful servant: thou hast been faithful over a few things, I will make thee ruler over many things: enter thou into the joy of thy lord.

Matthew 25:20, 21

The servant who received two talents was also pleased to be able to say, "Lord, thou deliveredst unto me two talents: behold, I have gained two other talents beside them." (Matthew 25:22)

The Lord also told him, "Well done."

The servant who received only one talent came to his master and said, "Lord, I knew thee that thou art an hard man. . . ." (Matthew 25:24)

"And I was afraid, and went and hid thy talent in the earth: lo, *there* thou hast *that is* thine. (Matthew 25:25)

His lord then rebuked him, saying, "Why did you bury your talent? Were you too lazy to try to use it? You knew I wanted you to improve the talent I gave you.

"If you had taken your talent to the marketplace, you could have made a profit. By this time you could have had not one but two talents."

The man knew in his heart he had behaved badly.

Then the master sorrowfully said, "Take therefore the talent from him, and give *it* unto him which hath ten talents." (Matthew 25:28)

Raising his voice in order for his servants to hear, the master told them that to everyone who uses his talents and makes them greater, he will give more talents. But for those who do not use their talents and bury them in the ground, from them shall be taken away even those talents which have been given them.

The master concluded by telling his servants that if they bury the talents he has given them, they are unprofitable servants and will be cast out. Then they will regret that they did not develop and use their talents.

As the family made its homeward journey, the father and oldest son again discussed the subject of talents.

The son spoke first, asking, "Father, Jesus wants me to develop my talents, doesn't he?"

"Yes, he does, my son. He wants you to learn to build the finest buildings in the world," replied the father. "Perhaps someday you will even have an opportunity to help build a beautiful building for God's people."

No more was said, but there were no idle thoughts on the remainder of that homeward journey.

THINK ABOUT IT:

1. What did the oldest son learn that he should do?
2. What are your talents? How can you develop and use your talents to help the Lord with his work?

37

FAITH MAKES IT POSSIBLE
Jesus Walks on the Sea

The disciples of Jesus could not sleep, even though it was well past midnight. As the ship they were on rolled from side to side and rose and fell with the waves, one of the disciples spoke, "I wish Jesus were here to calm this boiling sea as he did before."

"What will we do when he leaves us, as he says he must?" asked another of the disciples.

"We will use our talents just as he has taught us to do," Peter answered with a tone of confidence.

Suddenly a disciple, gazing out at the sea, shouted in astonishment, "Look!"

All turned and searched with their eyes in the direction the disciple pointed. "What is it?" shouted one, not trusting his own judgment of what he saw.

"It looks like a man," whispered another, who seemed too frightened to speak in a loud voice.

"It can't be a man," spoke a third. "No man could walk on the water like that. It must be a spirit."

As the form came closer, the disciples heard a voice they knew well, the voice of Jesus, saying, "Be of good cheer; it is I; be not afraid." (Matthew 14:27)

Peter stood silent for a moment and then called out, "Lord, . . . bid me come unto thee on the water." (Matthew 14:28)

The other disciples whispered among themselves, "Surely Peter would not dare try to walk on the water." Yet without a moment's delay Peter climbed down and began to walk toward Jesus.

However, as Peter was walking on the water, he became more aware of the wind and the waves about him. Slowly fear and doubt crept into his mind, and he began to flounder and sink into the dark, cold water. He cried out, "Lord, save me." (Matthew 14:30)

"And immediately Jesus stretched forth *his* hand, and caught him, and said unto him, O thou of little faith, wherefore didst thou doubt?" (Matthew 14:31)

With Jesus supporting him, Peter was able to return to the ship. The disciples reached down and helped both Peter and Jesus climb aboard. Suddenly the wind ceased, and all gathered closely around Jesus to worship him. They would never forget what they had seen that night on the storm-tossed sea. Each in his own words said to Jesus, "Of a truth thou art the Son of God." (Matthew 14:33)

In the many months that the disciples had walked, talked, and listened to Jesus, they had watched him meet his problems with calmness, power, courage, and wisdom. In other words, they had seen him walk on troubled waters many times. Athough in their hearts they knew he must soon leave them, each wondered, "Will we be able to carry on when he is gone? Or will we be like Peter and become frightened and sink into the waves that surround us? Will we have the faith we need?"

Indeed, there were turbulent storms ahead, for these men as well as for Jesus. The Savior would meet his challenges, and because of their faith in him, the disciples would also meet theirs.

THINK ABOUT IT:

1. What are you doing that you could do better if you had enough faith and weren't afraid?
2. How can you overcome your fears?

43

GREATNESS COMES IN HELPING OTHERS

James and John Request Honor

While the fame of Jesus spread, Jesus quietly continued his work. Although he knew that time was growing short, he realized there was still much to teach his disciples before he could leave them.

He must have been somewhat disappointed when two of his closest followers approached him one day with the request:

> Grant unto us that we may sit, one on thy right hand, and the other on thy left hand, in thy glory [when we are all in heaven].
>
> Mark 10:37

Jesus explained to these two men that even though they were among his most faithful followers, he could not make such a promise. He added that the great honor that they desired "... *shall be given to them* for whom it is prepared." (Mark 10:40)

Jesus then explained, ". . . whosoever will be great among you . . . shall be servant of all." (Mark 10:43, 44)

The disciples then understood that it is far better to serve others than to be served. True greatness is found in that person who goes among family and friends looking for ways to serve them, encourage them, and help them follow Jesus.

Jesus himself set the most perfect example of serving his fellowman. Soon he would become the servant of all by sacrificing his life in order that everyone might receive eternal life.

THE GOOD HOSTESS
Mary and Martha

Amidst his trials and hardships, Jesus had many pleasant moments. One such time was on a visit to the home of Mary and Martha. These two women lived not far from Jerusalem with their brother, Lazarus.

There was great excitement in this household over Jesus' visit. Upon his arrival, Jesus was greeted and made comfortable. Mary, sitting at Jesus' feet, said, "We are so happy that you are here. Please, tell us all that you have been doing and teach us more about the gospel."

While Jesus talked, Martha busily prepared dinner. Although she heard part of what Jesus was saying, she missed much of the message because she was hurrying about.

Feeling she couldn't manage everything by herself, Martha said to Jesus, "Lord, dost thou not care that my sister hath left me to serve alone? bid her therefore that she help me." (Luke 10:40)

Jesus could sense Martha's concern, but he wanted to teach her an important lesson. Gently he said,

Martha, Martha, thou art careful and troubled about many things [you are so worried about cooking a perfect meal and you are so busy preparing things]:

But one thing is needful: and Mary hath chosen that good part, which shall not be taken away from her [she wants to hear the gospel now because she knows she can eat later].

Luke 10:41, 42

Even though we may feel a little sorry for Martha, we should remember the lesson Jesus taught here, that when we have an opportunity to hear the teachings of Jesus, we should put other things aside.

LET US ALL BE GRATEFUL
Healing of the Lepers

Jesus spent his entire life serving others. Yet there were many who did not thank him for his help.

As Jesus and his disciples neared the gate of a certain city, they heard a group of men shouting at a distance. Jesus turned to hear what the men were saying and heard their plea: "Jesus, Master, have mercy on us." (Luke 17:13)

A man coming through the gate saw what was happening and said in a warning tone, "Stay away from those men. They are sick with the terrible disease of leprosy. If you look closely, you can see the sores all over their bodies."

Jesus knew even before this man had spoken that this was a group of lepers. There were many at this time who were stricken with this dreaded disease from which there was no cure.

Jesus' heart was touched that these men had enough faith to ask him for help. In a loud voice he called out to them, "Go shew yourselves unto the priests." (Luke 17:14) Upon hearing the words of Jesus, the lepers hurried off to see the priests.

As the lepers entered the city gate, they felt their bodies healing. Soon one shouted, "I'm healed, I'm cleansed." The others joined in, "And so are we."

When the ten showed themselves to the priests, the leaders were amazed. They discovered that all ten lepers were completely cured and pronounced them clean.

Nine of the lepers went their separate ways. But one, a Samaritan, felt he must find Jesus and thank him for healing his leprosy. Returning to Jesus, he fell down on his knees and cried tears of joy and gratitude. Jesus, knowing who the man was, asked, "Were there not ten cleansed? but where *are* the nine?" (Luke 17:17)

Jesus then lifted the man up and said, 'Arise, go thy way: thy faith hath made thee whole." (Luke 17:19)

Some disciples of Jesus who overheard this scene felt ashamed there had been so few willing to thank Jesus. Each of them personally resolved to be among those who did.

A GREAT SADNESS
John Is Beheaded

During the three years of Jesus' ministry among men, Jesus and John the Baptist were seldom together. Although John went to different places than Jesus, he preached the same principles that Jesus taught. He reminded the people to follow the teachings of Jesus, and he always bore testimony that Jesus was the Son of God and the Savior of the world.

Because of what John preached, Satan prompted a wicked king named Herod to have John arrested and thrown into prison. While in prison John longed to hear of the work Jesus was doing. Calling two of his friends to him, he asked them to find Jesus and then return and tell him what they had seen and heard.

Upon finding Jesus, John's two friends told him who had sent them. Jesus had them return to John with this message:

> . . . tell John what things ye have seen and heard; how that the blind see, the lame walk, the lepers are cleansed, the deaf hear, the dead are raised, to the poor the gospel is preached.

Luke 7:22

After the men had departed, Jesus testified to those who were with him that John was much more than a prophet.

This is *he*, of whom it is written, Behold, I send my messenger before thy face, which shall prepare thy way before thee.

For I say unto you, Among those that are born of women there is not a greater prophet than John the Baptist. . . .

Luke 7:27, 28

John had been put into prison because he had accused King Herod of being a sinner. Herod had not only been unfaithful to his own wife, but he was living with his brother's wife as well. The truth in John's accusation had angered the king, but he didn't dare harm John because he was revered as a prophet by so many people.

On Herod's birthday there was a great celebration. Herodias, the woman with whom Herod was living, didn't like John because of what he had told Herod. At the party she asked Herod, "Would you like it if my daughter danced for you?"

"Oh, yes," replied Herod. "I would like that very much. She is a beautiful woman and a wonderful dancer."

When the young woman had finished dancing, Herod was greatly pleased. He beckoned for her to come over to where he was sitting and then said to her, "Your dance was the best I have seen. I will give you whatever it is you desire most."

Having been instructed by her mother beforehand, the daughter spoke loudly and without hesitation, "Give me here John Baptist's head in a charger [large plate]." (Matthew 14:8)

And the king was sorry [he was afraid of what the people would do]: nevertheless for the oath's sake . . . he commanded *it* to be given *her*.

And he sent, and beheaded John in the prison.

And his head was brought . . . and given to the damsel: and she brought *it* to her mother.

And his disciples came, and took up the body, and buried it, and went and told Jesus.

Matthew 14:9-12

Jesus was deeply saddened when he learned of John's death. In order to be alone he boarded a boat and crossed the water to a desert shore. But people followed him there as well. Upon seeing a multitude of his followers, Jesus' heart was filled with great love for them. After healing their sick, he preached the gospel to all.

John, the greatest prophet to be born of women, the one who had baptized Jesus, the one whom Jesus had loved deeply, was now gone from the earth to his reward in heaven.

THINK ABOUT IT:

Why do you think Jesus was willing to accept great sadness in his life?

THE SON OF GOD
Peter Testifies

As Jesus and his disciples entered a certain city, they saw a small group of people coming toward them, leading a blind man. The man holding the blind man's arm said, "Master, this man is blind. Please heal him and make him able to see."

Jesus, beckoning the group to follow him, walked back out of the city and down a winding road. Finally he paused, and the others gathered around him.

Facing the blind man, Jesus placed his own finger to his lips and moistened it. Then he gently rubbed the moisture on each of the blind man's eyelids. After this he asked the man if he could see.

The blind man looked up and said,

. . . I see men as trees, walking.
　　After that he [Jesus] put *his* hands again upon his eyes, and made him look up:
and he was restored, and saw every man clearly.

Mark 8:24, 25

Jesus told the grateful man not to tell anyone about what had happened. Because of the jealousy growing among the religious leaders, the less said about his miracles the better.

With thoughts of this latest miracle running through his mind, Peter walked by Jesus as they journeyed throughout Caesarea Philippi. Along the way Jesus asked his disciples, "Whom do men say that I the Son of man am?" (Matthew 16:13)

One answered, "Some say you are John the Baptist come back to life. Others say you are one of the other prophets."

Jesus repeated his question to them, "But whom say ye that I am?" (Matthew 16:15)

Peter, who had been deep in thought since Jesus had first asked the question, could restrain himself no longer. In a firm but sincere voice he said, "Thou are the Christ, the Son of the living God." (Matthew 16:16)

Although Peter could remember all of Jesus' miracles, there was something in his soul that went beyond what he had seen and heard. His testimony came from a still, small voice that whispered to his heart that Jesus was the Son of God.

Jesus was pleased with Peter's answer. He was now confident that Peter was ready to bear his testimony to the world when the time came.

God, our Heavenly Father, had revealed Jesus' identity to Peter through the Holy Ghost. Likewise, he will reveal this truth to every person who truly seeks to know his Son, Jesus Christ.

THINK ABOUT IT:

1. Have you ever heard a still, small voice whisper to you that Jesus is the Son of God?
2. How should we live in order that this can happen?

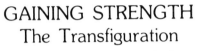

GAINING STRENGTH
The Transfiguration

From that time forth began Jesus to shew unto his disciples, how that he must go unto Jerusalem, and suffer many things of the elders and chief priests and scribes, and be killed, and be raised again the third day.

Matthew 16:21

Although victory lay ahead, the path would be difficult. Jesus was going to need great strength, and there was still work to be done.

Taking with him only Peter, James, and John, Jesus went to a high mountain. After climbing to a place where he knew they were alone, the four of them knelt down together and Jesus began to pray.

The Bible tells us that as Jesus prayed, he

> was transfigured [changed] before them: and his face did shine as the sun, and his raiment [clothing] was white as the light.

Matthew 17:2

As Peter, James, and John silently looked on, they were somewhat startled to see two other heavenly men standing near Jesus. As they listened, they learned that these two men were Moses and Elias, two prophets who had lived centuries earlier. The three men were discussing Jesus' death that would soon take place at Jerusalem.

After the departure of Moses and Elias,

> . . . a bright cloud overshadowed them: and behold a voice out of the cloud, which said, This is my beloved Son, in whom I am well pleased; hear ye him.

Matthew 17:5

Peter, James, and John knew that the voice they had heard was that of God, the Eternal Father. This experience strengthened their testimonies of Jesus' true lineage.

Being so close to God and hearing his voice was more than the three disciples could bear and

. . . they fell on their face, and were sore afraid.

And Jesus came and touched them, and said, Arise, and be not afraid.

And when they had lifted up their eyes, they saw no man, save Jesus only.

Matthew 17:6-8

Jesus had received great strength from these two experiences. He now felt prepared to walk into the valley of the shadow of death, and he knew his Heavenly Father would be with him.

As the four weary but inspired men made their way down the steep mountain, the disciples said very little. Jesus paused and turned to face the other three in the group, saying, "Tell the vision to no man, until the Son of man be risen again from the dead." (Matthew 17:9)

Peter, James, and John each consented, but later they asked each other, "What did he mean about rising from the dead?" Although the disciples had a faint idea of the future, they did not fully understand that Jesus would die and then come back to life, or be resurrected. Yet, knowing that he was the Son of God, they knew that whatever Jesus said would surely come to pass.

At a later time, after the death and resurrection of Jesus, these apostles would tell others of the significant events of that glorious day on the mountain, when Jesus had been transfigured before them.

THINK ABOUT IT:

1. In what ways does this story help us to love the Lord more?
2. What is the best way for us to gain strength when we face difficult tasks or experiences?

GOD WILL PROVIDE
The Tribute Money

Knowing full well how the scribes and Pharisees hated Jesus, the disciples must have often asked Jesus, "Master, what can we do to protect you? Is there any way we can help you?"

And while they abode in Galilee, Jesus said unto them, The Son of man shall be betrayed into the hands of men:

And they shall kill him, and the third day he shall be raised again. . . .

Matthew 17:22, 23

Although the disciples did not yet fully understand, they were afraid to ask him any more questions.

As Jesus and his disciples were visiting at Capernaum, a man appointed to collect tribute money asked Peter, "Does your master pay tribute?"

Peter answered him yes, but feeling somewhat confused over whether he had given an honest answer, he later asked Jesus about the matter.

Jesus explained to Peter that tribute money was used to help the work of the Lord. Therefore, because Jesus was the Son of God, he should not be required to pay.

As Peter turned to go, Jesus called out,

Notwithstanding, lest we should offend them, go thou to the sea, and cast an hook, and take up the fish that first cometh up; and when thou hast opened his mouth, thou shalt find a piece of money: that take, and give unto them for me and thee.

Matthew 17:27

JESUS CAME TO SAVE, NOT TO DESTROY
The Samaritan Village

Jesus knew that his time among men was growing shorter. Against the wishes of some of his disciples, they began their journey southward toward Jerusalem. As they traveled through Samaria, it began to grow dark and they looked for a place to spend the night. But the Samaritans did not want these Jews to stay in their city.

> And when his disciples James and John saw *this*, they said, Lord, wilt thou that we command fire to come down from heaven, and consume them . . . ?

Luke 9:54

Even though these men knew of Jesus' power, they did not understand the feelings of his heart. As they awaited his answer to destroy one and all, Jesus "rebuked them, and said, Ye know not what manner of spirit ye are

of." (Luke 9:55) They then realized that it was Satan, not Jesus, who was set on destroying people. Jesus then added,

> For the Son of man is not come to destroy men's lives, but to save *them*. And they went to another village.
>
> Luke 9:56

SOME BELIEVE; OTHERS DON'T
Jesus Teaches in the Temple

By this time all the people had heard of Jesus.

> And there was much murmuring among the people concerning him: for some said, He is a good man: others said, Nay; but he deceiveth the people.
>
> John 7:12

Many of those who did believe Jesus was the promised Messiah dared not speak openly about it because they feared the religious leaders.

When Jesus arrived at Jerusalem, a huge celebration called the Feast of Tabernacles was being held. Jesus went directly to the temple and began to teach. The people gathered around him, and some of the religious leaders were among the crowd. As these leaders listened to Jesus, they were amazed at his wisdom and knowledge of the scriptures. One asked another,

> How knoweth this man letters, having never learned?
> Jesus answered them, and said, My doctrine is not mine, but his that sent me.
> If any man will do his will, he shall know of the doctrine, whether it be of God, or *whether* I speak of myself.
>
> John 7:15-17

As Jesus continued teaching, the scribes and Pharisees tried to trick him with questions and show his listeners he was not the Son of God. Although some were now convinced that Jesus was the promised Messiah, there were others who would have had him arrested if they had not feared it would cause an uprising from the people.

THINK ABOUT IT:

Why do you think that some believed in Jesus and others didn't?

WISDOM WINS
The Woman Who Sinned

The next day Jesus returned to the temple and once again began to teach. Suddenly there was a commotion, as a group of men appeared dragging a woman by her arms. Accompanying this group were scribes and Pharisees who wanted to find evidence against Jesus to arrest him.

As the men threw the woman in front of Jesus, a scribe shouted, "Master, this woman has sinned and broken one of our most important laws." Jesus watched the crying woman, as the scribe continued, "Now Moses in the law commanded us, that such should be stoned. . . . " (John 8:5)

After a brief pause the man continued, "You seem to know so much. What do you say, Master? What should we do to her?"

The evil men then waited for an answer. They knew that to kill her was not what Jesus wanted nor taught. However, if Jesus told them to disobey the law of Moses, they could arrest him for his disobedience.

As the rebellious crowd waited impatiently for an answer, the man again asked Jesus what they should do. Finally, looking up from where he had been writing in the dirt with his finger, Jesus said, "He that is without sin among you, let him first cast a stone at her." (John 8:7)

There was silence, and Jesus once again stooped down and wrote on the ground. One by one the people, remembering their own sins, quietly began to leave. Finally Jesus was left alone with the woman.

When Jesus had lifted up himself, and saw none but the woman, he said unto her, Woman, where are those thine accusers? hath no man condemned thee?

She said, No man, Lord. And Jesus said unto her, Neither do I condemn thee: go, and sin no more.

John 8:10, 11

Although their attempt to arrest Jesus had failed again, the scribes and Pharisees continued their plots against Jesus.

THINK ABOUT IT:

Why was Jesus so wise in the things that he did and said?

TESTIFYING OF HIM
The Man Born Blind

The Jewish people had strict laws about what could or could not be done on the Sabbath. It was on this holy day that Jesus' disciples brought a man who had been blind since birth. After looking at the man for a moment, Jesus knelt down and rubbed some of his spit into the soil. Then, molding the moistened soil into clay with his fingers, he anointed the eyes of the blind man with the clay by applying it over the man's eyelids.

Jesus then said to the man, "Go and wash your eyes in the pool of Siloam."

The man ran quickly to the pool and did as Jesus had told him. Moments later he shouted, "I can see!"

Running here and there, he shouted to everyone he passed, "I can see!" Some who saw the man said, "Isn't this the fellow that was born blind?" Others said, "It looks like him, but it can't be!"

The man then explained to them how Jesus had anointed his eyes, how he had followed Jesus' instructions to wash, and how he was then able to see. This account of his healing spread to nearby cities and villages.

When the scribes and Pharisees heard of what had happened, they sent for the man who had been born blind. As he stood before them, they demanded, "Tell us what happened!"

After he had repeated his story to them, one asked, "You mean he did this on the Sabbath?" Another, who did not believe the story, said, "This is a trick. You've always been able to see."

After the parents of the blind man had been sent for, they were asked,

Is this your son, who ye say was born blind? how then doth he now see?

John 9:19

His parents answered them and said, We know that this is our son, and that he was born blind:

But by what means he now seeth, we know not; or who hath opened his eyes, we know not: he is of age; ask him: he shall speak for himself.

John 9:20, 21

The parents were afraid that a more complete answer would anger the religous leaders and get themselves into trouble.

The son was again asked if he'd been given his sight by a sinner—a person who did not keep the Sabbath day holy.

He answered and said, Whether he be a sinner *or no*, I know not: one thing I know, that, whereas I was blind, now I *see.*

Then said they to him again, What did he to thee? how opened he thine *eyes?*

He answered them, I have told you already, and ye did not hear: wherefore would ye hear *it* again? will ye also be his disciples?

Then they reviled him, and said, Thou art
his disciple; but *we* are Moses' disciples.

We know that God spake unto Moses: *as
for* this *fellow*, we know not from whence he is.

John 9:25-29

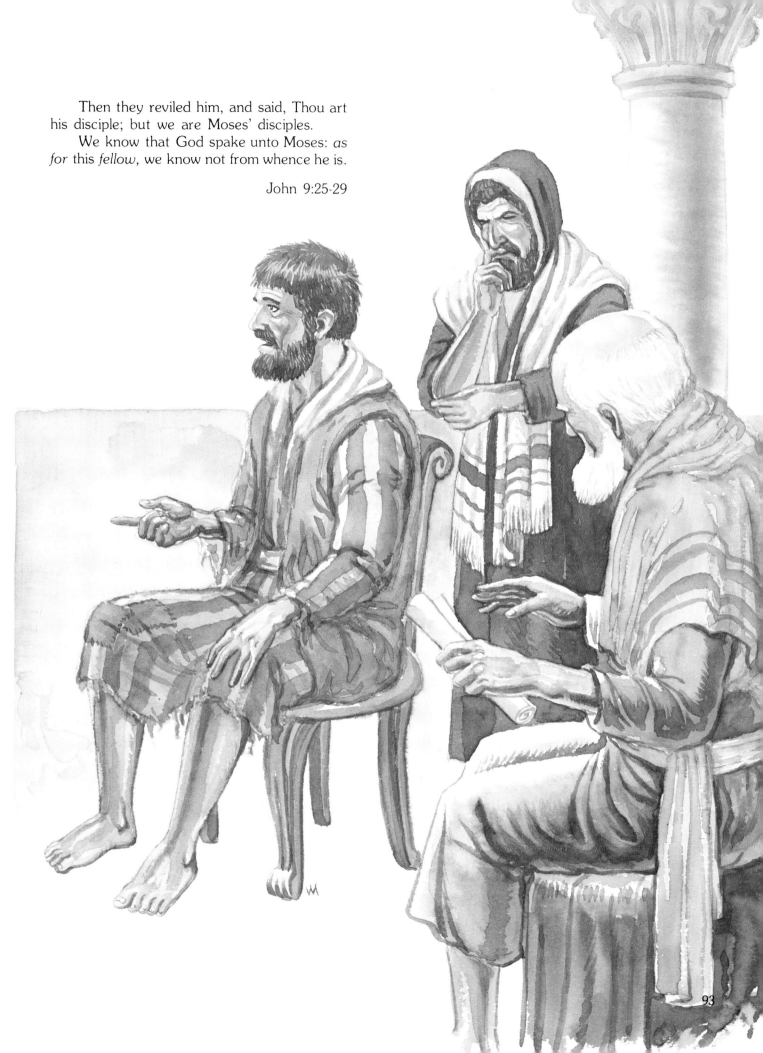

By this time the Pharisees were deeply angered, and they cast the man out of their church and told him not to return.

When Jesus learned of this, he went to the man and asked,

Dost thou believe on the Son of God?

He answered and said, Who is he, Lord, that I might believe on him?

And Jesus said unto him, Thou hast both seen him, and it is he that talketh with thee.

And he said, Lord, I believe. And he worshipped him.

John 9:35-38

THINK ABOUT IT:

What is an important lesson we can learn from this blind man who was healed by Jesus?

THE TESTIMONY OF JESUS
Accused of Blasphemy

Although those who hated Jesus felt he was guilty of violating
the Sabbath, they also realized they needed more than this to arrest

him. If only he would clearly state that he was the Son of God, they could charge him with blasphemy, the penalty for which was death.

With this thought of trickery in mind, some of the Jews came to him and said,

How long dost thou make us to doubt? If thou be the Christ, tell us plainly.

John 10:24

Jesus answered them, I told you, and
ye believed not: the works that I do in my
Father's name, they bear witness of me.
I and *my* Father are one.

John 10:25, 30

In anger they replied,

For a good work we stone thee not; but for
blasphemy; and because that thou, being a
man, makest thyself God.

John 10:33

After this conversation they tried to
take him away, but he escaped again.

IT ISN'T EASY
Count the Cost

Jesus was warned that not only were the scribes and Pharisees attempting to arrest him, but also that King Herod had threatened to kill him unless he left Jerusalem. However, Jesus had no fear of this evil man who had murdered his friend, John the Baptist. He told those who had warned him,

> Go ye, and tell that fox, . . . it cannot be that a prophet perish out of Jerusalem.
>
> Luke 13:32, 33

It was about this time that Jesus heard Lazarus, the brother of Mary and Martha, was very ill. His disciples were surprised when he did not leave for Bethany immediately but instead remained where he was, preaching and healing the sick. Once again Jesus healed a man on the Sabbath, and once again the Jewish leaders were angry.

In response to their accusations Jesus said,

> Which of you shall have an ass or an ox fallen into a pit, and will not straightway pull him out on the sabbath day?
> And they could not answer him again to these things.
>
> Luke 14:5, 6

By this time great multitudes followed Jesus. Teaching these followers, he said, "And whosoever doth not bear his cross, and come after me, cannot be my disciple." (Luke 14:27)

Jesus continued,

For which of you, intending to build a tower, sitteth not down first, and counteth the cost, whether he have *sufficient* to finish *it?*

Lest haply, after he hath laid the foundation, and is not able to finish *it,* all that behold *it* begin to mock him,

Saying, This man began to build, and was not able to finish.

Luke 14:28-30

It takes courage and a strong will to follow Jesus. He gives us much and he expects us to give him much in return. However, the sacrifices are small when compared to the blessings we receive for our good works.

THINK ABOUT IT:

1. What would you like to achieve in the next year?
2. What will you have to sacrifice in order to reach your goals?

POWER OVER DEATH
The Raising of Lazarus

Several days had passed since Jesus had first learned of the illness of Lazarus. When he finally came near Bethany, Lazarus had been dead for some time. Some of Mary and Martha's friends saw Jesus coming and told the two sorrowing sisters.

Then Martha, as soon as she heard that Jesus was coming, went and met him: but Mary sat *still* in the house.

Then said Martha unto Jesus, Lord, if thou hadst been here, my brother had not died.

But I know, that even now, whatsoever thou wilt ask of God, God will give *it* thee.

Jesus saith unto her, Thy brother shall rise again.

Martha saith unto him, I know that he shall rise again in the resurrection at the last day.

Jesus said unto her, I am the resurrection, and the life: he that believeth in me, though he were dead, yet shall he live:

And whosoever liveth and believeth in me shall never die. . . .

John 11:20-26

After talking to Jesus, Martha returned to the house, where Mary was. She gently said, "The Master is here, and he has asked to see you."

Mary quickly arose and went to him.

> Then when Mary was come where Jesus was, and saw him, she fell down at his feet, saying unto him, Lord, if thou hadst been here, my brother had not died.
>
> John 11:32

Mary was weeping as she spoke. Jesus, feeling troubled, gently asked, "Where did you lay him?"

As Jesus followed Mary, he wept. Those who watched said, "Behold how he loved him!" (John 11:36)

Others said, "We have heard so much about how he opens the eyes of the blind. Couldn't he have kept this man from dying as well?"

Lazarus' grave was a cave with a large stone covering the entrance. Jesus asked that the stone be moved aside. Martha, wondering what Jesus was going to do, reminded him that her brother had been dead for four days.

> Jesus saith unto her, Said I not unto thee, that, if thou wouldest believe, thou shouldest see the glory of God?
>
> John 11:40

After praying to his Father, Jesus said in a loud voice,

> Lazarus, come forth.
>
> And he that was dead came forth, bound hand and foot with graveclothes: and his face was bound about with a napkin. Jesus saith unto them, Loose him, and let him go.
>
> John 11:43, 44

> Then many of the Jews which came to Mary, and had seen the things which Jesus did, believed on him.
>
> But some of them went their ways to the Pharisees, and told them what things Jesus had done.
>
> John 11:45, 46

This was Jesus' last miracle before his crucifixion. It almost seemed like a preview of Christ himself dying and rising again. Death had lost its sting, and the grave and Satan were about to lose their victory.

Soon all the people had heard the news of Lazarus being brought back to life. The story of the blind man receiving his sight had been hard for the Jewish leaders to accept, but to be able to raise a man who had already been dead for four days was unbelievable to them. They felt they must act soon or it would be too late to do anything at all against Jesus.

THINK ABOUT IT:

How does the raising of Lazarus preview what was soon to come?

FOLLOW HIM
The Rich Ruler

A husband spoke quietly to his wife so as not to awaken their eight-year-old son, who they thought was sleeping: "Today I overheard two Pharisees speaking in the marketplace. One said that Caiaphas the high priest is angry with Jesus for his recent miracles and feels he must be stopped before all the people believe in him. Caiaphas says that if everyone were to believe in Jesus, the Romans would become angry and destroy us all."

The wife replied, "The priests are not afraid of the Romans. Instead, they are jealous of Jesus because he raised Lazarus from the dead, and they fear his power over all the people. Today when the rich

man asked Jesus what he must do, Jesus told him to keep the commandments. When the rich man said he already did, Jesus told him to sell all that he had, give his money to the poor, and follow him."

"And yet the rich man turned away," commented the husband. "Jesus did not have much power over him."

"Let us hope that we would not have turned away," responded the wife. "We must follow him at all cost."

Suddenly the parents were startled to hear their son's voice, "I would not have turned away from him, Mother. Today when the disciples asked me and the other children to step back and not bother Jesus, he rebuked them and said, 'Suffer little children, and forbid them not, to come unto me: for of such is the kingdom of heaven.' (Matthew 19:14) Then he laid his hands on us and blessed us."

"Yes, we remember well," confirmed the mother. "There are many people who love Jesus because they feel his love for them. Let us hope that he can stay with us and be our king. But now it is time to go to sleep."

_____

THINK ABOUT IT:

Why do you think Jesus loved children so much?

THE KING
The Triumphant Entry

It had been thirty-three years since Jesus' birth. There remained just one week before he would die. Although at first it might appear that Jesus' death would be a victory for Satan, it would actually signal the defeat of what Satan hoped to achieve. For in dying, Jesus would open the door of eternal life for every man, woman, and child who ever lives on this earth.

On the first day of this last week in Jesus' mortal life, Jesus was finishing his work in the smaller villages near Jerusalem. Although the Jewish leaders were not always certain where he was, they knew he was heading toward Jerusalem.

As Jesus and his disciples neared the city walls, he sent two disciples ahead on an essential errand. As the two hurried ahead, one spoke, "He promised us that we would find a colt (donkey) tied up with a rope around its neck."

The other confirmed, "And there it is. Jesus promised us it would be so young that no man would have ever ridden upon it."

As they were untying the donkey, a man asked them, "What are you doing? That is my young donkey!"

The disciples remembered what Jesus had told them to tell the owner. One spoke, ". . . the Lord hath need of him. . . . " (Mark 11:3)

At first the man didn't seem to understand, but then he sensed their mission and said, "You may take him to the Lord."

The disciples quickly led the colt back to where Jesus was waiting.

When Jesus announced that he would ride the animal into the Holy City, the disciples quickly cast some of their robes on the donkey's back. This being done, Jesus mounted and began the journey into Jerusalem.

As Jesus entered the city, rows of people formed on each side of him. Many spread their garments along the road so that the donkey could walk on the soft clothing.

> . . . and others cut down branches off the [palm] trees, and strawed *them* in the way.
>
> And they that went before, and they that followed, cried, saying, Hosanna; Blessed *is* he that cometh in the name of the Lord:
>
> Blessed *be* the kingdom of our father David, that cometh in the name of the Lord: Hosanna in the highest.
>
> Mark 11:8-10

And Jesus entered into Jerusalem, and into the temple: and when he had looked round about upon all things, and now the eventide was come, he went out unto Bethany with the twelve.

Mark 11:11

The crowds had been enormous that day. When the leaders had asked Jesus to tell the people to go home to prevent trouble, Jesus had not done so. He had said,

I tell you that, if these [people] should hold their peace, the stones would immediately cry out.

Luke 19:40

This day had been one of triumph for Jesus. The people had recognized him as their King. Even the Pharisees had whispered one to another, ". . . behold, the world is gone after him." (John 12:19)

THINK ABOUT IT:

1. Do you think Christ could have become an earthly king if he had so desired?
2. Why didn't he care about earthly honor and power?

As Jesus entered the temple yard, he was angered to see people buying, selling, and changing money in his Father's house. Without warning Jesus hurried from table to table, overturning each one. Money flew in every direction. As the money changers moved back to avoid being hit, they heard Jesus call out,

It is written, My house shall be called the house of prayer; but ye have made it a den of thieves.

Matthew 21:13

COURAGE BEYOND COMPARE
Jesus Cleanses the Temple

After spending the night in the city of Bethany, which was located about two miles outside Jerusalem, Jesus arose early and once again journeyed into the city.

This time, making his way on foot, he headed straight for the temple. As he drew near, he heard voices crying out, "Doves for sale! Get them here! Lowest prices in the temple! They make perfect temple offerings!"

Moments later the temple yard was silent. This time no one challenged what Jesus had done, for even the Pharisees knew in their hearts that Jesus was right.

Shortly after this incident the blind and the lame came to Jesus, and he healed them and taught those around him about the gospel. That evening he again returned to Bethany.

What a powerful example Jesus set by refusing to watch others defile the house of God. He took action and, because he was right, no man could stand in his way.

THINK ABOUT IT:

Why did the religious leaders allow Jesus to do what he did at the temple?

WISDOM COMES FROM BEING RIGHT
By What Authority?

On the third day Jesus returned again to the temple at Jerusalem. There were still lessons to be taught and time was running out.

Once in the temple Jesus began to teach. A Pharisee, who was one of the chief priests, got the attention of Jesus and asked, "Yesterday you came here and caused a great deal of damage by turning over the tables of the money changers. After considering this serious matter, we want to ask you,"

By what authority doest thou these things? and who gave thee this authority?

And Jesus answered and said unto them, I also will ask you one thing, which if ye tell me, I in like wise will tell you by what authority I do these things.

The baptism of John, whence was it? from heaven, or of men? And they reasoned with themselves, saying, If we shall say, From heaven; he will say unto us, Why did ye not then believe him?

But if we shall say, Of men; we fear the people; for all hold John as a prophet.

And they answered Jesus, and said, We cannot tell. And he said unto them, Neither tell I you by what authority I do these things.

Matthew 21:23-27

This answer angered the Pharisees because they knew they had failed at trapping Jesus into saying that he received his authority from God. If he had said that, they could have accused him of blasphemy and had him arrested.

Jesus then began a parable about a rich man who planted a vineyard, after which he went into a far country. When it was harvest time, he told his servants to return and pick the grapes of his vineyard.

Those living near the vineyard met the servants and beat the first, killed the next, and stoned another. Other servants were sent, and they too were beaten, killed, or stoned. Finally the rich man sent his own son, and the wicked people killed him as well.

Jesus then asked, "When the lord therefore of the vineyard cometh, what will he do unto those husbandmen [farmers]?" (Matthew 21:40)

Someone nearby responded, "He will miserably destroy those wicked men and will let out *his* vineyard unto other husbandmen. . . ." (Matthew 21:41)

And when the chief priests and Pharisees had heard his parables, they perceived that he spake of them.

But when they sought to lay hands on him, they feared the multitude, because they took him for a prophet.

Matthew 21:45, 46

When prophets had come in years past—Jeremiah, Isaiah, Hosea, and others—the people had beaten, killed, or stoned them. Now the very Son of God had been sent to God's earthly vineyard. Soon the chief priests would have him killed also, for Satan had control of their hearts.

131

PREVIEW OF THINGS TO COME

Volume Ten will complete our stories of the Bible. In it we will read of Jesus' death, his resurrection, and how the Twelve Apostles carried on with his work.

The resurrection of Christ gives hope to all people. Our knowledge of this first Easter makes us aware of the fact that, because Christ the Lord has risen, we will all live again. Mortal death has lost its sting.

Peter, Paul, John, and many others knew that Jesus Christ had arisen from the dead. They had no doubt of this fact and wanted all people everywhere to know this same truth. For this purpose they set out to preach the glorious news to all the world.

Yes, in Volume Ten we will see how the message was spread that Jesus lived, died, and lives again. This knowledge will increase our testimony of Jesus' unequaled sacrifice for us.